Native American Leaders

by

Janet Hubbard–Brown

Chelsea House Publishers
Philadelphia

CHELSEA HOUSE PUBLISHERS

Editor-in-Chief Stephen Reginald
Managing Editor James D. Gallagher
Production Manager Pamela Loos
Art Director Sara Davis
Picture Editor Judy Hasday
Senior Production Editor Lisa Chippendale
Designer Takeshi Takahashi

First Printing

1 3 5 7 9 8 6 4 2

Library of Congress Cataloging-in-Publication Data

Hubbard-Brown, Janet.
Native American leaders / by Janet Hubbard-Brown.

p. cm. — (Costume, tradition, and culture: reflecting on
the past))
Includes bibliographical references and index.
Summary: Profiles twenty-five Native American leaders,
mostly from the nineteenth century, including Big Elk
(Omaha), Geronimo (Apache), Joseph (Nez Perce), Red
Cloud (Oglala Sioux), and White Swan (Crow).

ISBN 0-7910-5209-5 (hardcover)
1. Indians of North America—Biography—Juvenile litera-
ture. [1. Indians of North America—Biography.] I. Title.
II. Series.
E89.H87 1998   98-31352
970.004—dc21   CIP
                                                        AC

CONTENTS

꙳

INTRODUCTION

For as long as people have known that other cultures existed, they have been curious about the differences in their customs and traditions. Julius Caesar, the famous Roman leader, wrote long chronicles about the inhabitants of Gaul (modern-day France) while he was leading troops in the Gallic Wars (58–51 B.C.). In the chronicles, he discussed their religious beliefs, their customs, their day-to-day life, and the conflicts among the different groups. Explorers like Marco Polo traveled thousands of miles and devoted years of their lives to learning about the peoples of the East and bringing home the stories of Chinese court life, along with the silks, spices, and inventions of that culture. The Chelsea House series *Costume, Tradition, and Culture: Reflecting on the Past* continues this legacy of exploration and discovery by discussing some of the most fascinating traditions, beliefs, legends, and artifacts from around the world.

Different cultures develop traditions and costumes to mark the roles of people in their societies, to commemorate events in their histories, and to make the changes and mysteries of life more meaningful. Soldiers wear uniforms to show that they are serving in their nation's army, and insignia on the uniforms show what ranks they hold within the army. People of Bukhara, a city in Uzbekistan, have for centuries woven fine threads of gold into their clothes, and when they travel to other cities they can be recognized as Bukharans by the golden embroidery on their traditional costume. For many years, in the Irish countryside, people would leave bowls of milk outside at night as an offering to the fairies, or "Good People," believing that this would help ensure their favor and keep the family safe from fairy mischief. In Mexico, November 2 is the Day of the Dead, when people visit cemeteries and have feasts to remember their ancestors. In the United States, brides wear white dresses, and the traditional wedding includes many rituals: the father of the bride "giving her away" to the groom, the exchange of vows and rings, the throwing of rice, the tossing of the bride's bouquet. These rituals and symbols help make the marriage meaningful and special for the couple, their families, and their friends, by expressing the change that is taking place and allowing the friends and families to wish luck to the couple.

This series will explore some of the myths, symbols, costumes, and traditions of various cultures from around the world and different times in the past. *Fighting Units of the American War of Independence,* for example, will detail the uniforms, weapons, and decorations of the regiments and battalions on both sides of the war, along with the battles in which they became famous. *Roman Myths, Heroes, and Legends* describes how the ancient Romans explained the wonders and natural phenomena of their world with fantastic stories of superhuman heroes and almost human deities who could change the course of history at will. In *Popular Superstitions,* you will learn how some familiar superstitious beliefs—such as throwing spilled salt over your shoulder, or hanging a horseshoe over your door for good luck—originally began, in times when people feared that devils and evil spirits were meddling in their lives. Few people still believe in malicious spirits, but many still toss the spilled salt over their shoulders, or knock on wood when expressing cautious hope. The legendary figures of a culture—the brave explorers of *The Wild West* or the wicked brigands described in *Infamous Pirates*— help shape that culture's values by providing grand, almost mythical examples of what people should (or should not!) strive to be.

The illustrations that accompany these books have their own cultural history. Originally, they were printed on small collectors' cards and sold in the early 20th century. Each card in a set of 25 or 50 would depict a different person, artifact, or event, and usually the reverse side would offer a few sentences of description to explain the picture. Now, they provide a fascinating glimpse into history and an entertaining addition to the stories presented here.

ABOUT THE AUTHOR

JANET HUBBARD-BROWN is the author of a dozen books for children and young adults. She is also a freelance editor and researcher. She lives in Vermont with her husband and two children.

Chelsea House Publishers and the author are indebted to Suad McCoy for all the research she did on this project.

OVERVIEW
Leaders and Their Tribes

Photographers who came to take pictures of Native Americans from 1840 on were called "shadow catchers" by the Plains Indians. They thought the photographs captured a part of them and gave the viewer power over them.

The Native American leaders in this book are warriors, statesmen, orators, pacifists, and schemers. In other words, they are a cross-section of humanity—from Sitting Bull, who led thousands against the whites after his tribe's land, and who died resisting his captors, to John Grass, a reservation police chief who became a leader, partly because of how adaptable to the white culture he was.

Photo archivists at the Smithsonian Institution in Washington, D.C., have had to put together a collection of Native American photographs that came to them misdated and misidentified. It is often even more difficult for researchers to find biographical documentation about many of the subjects of the photographs, because most of Native American history is oral.

The chief of a tribe or band was not an absolute monarch. He came into his position of power through his achievements, usually in warfare with neighboring enemies, and through his acquired wisdom. He exercised a powerful influence over the tribe as a whole and gave advice when needed.

All the leaders here were confronted with overwhelming changes as white settlers moved onto their land. Land to the

Native Americans was not real estate or a source of profit as it was to the whites. It was a direct source of life. Land was also a way of life; the Native Americans adapted themselves to the land rather than shaping their environment to fit their way of life. With such opposing points of view, many feel that war between whites and Indians could not have been avoided.

The Native Americans had been accustomed to fighting man against man. War with the whites changed the numbers and the weapons. Replacements for whites killed in battle seemed endless to the Native Americans, and the sophisticated weapons the whites brought added a new dimension to war. Eventually, through diseases that wiped out entire communities, and through constant warfare either with the whites or among themselves, the Native American tribes succumbed to the white takeover.

In the end, most of the chiefs included here suffered defeat, for defeat includes the loss of a way of life. What was written about Sitting Bull could also be said of many of these chiefs, after the coming of the whites: "Sitting Bull had nine years of life left to him. They were strange years, often desolate, now and then lighted by sparks of defiance, burdened with a constant weight of mortification. But some quality of the chief's spirit seemed to lift him above humiliation, leaving the essence of the man untarnished."

ARIKÍTA, OTOE

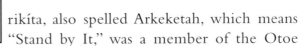

Arikíta, also spelled Arkeketah, which means "Stand by It," was a member of the Otoe tribe, a tribe of Sioux farmers and hunters who settled in Nebraska. They had at one time joined with the Winnebago group and with the Missouri Indians but eventually split from both. The Otoes were not a prominent tribe, and when Lewis and Clark visited them in 1804 they found the tribe already in poor condition.

Arikíta had a reputation among his people as a schemer. Once, when Pawnees attacked a trainload of emigrants on Big Sandy Creek, Nebraska, and robbed them of all their belongings, Arikíta and his band of followers killed all the Pawnees. The whites praised him, of course, and he received letters commending his performance. But his own people were not so admiring.

Arikíta became head chief of the Otoes while on a visit to Washington, when the Otoes signed away the southeastern part of Nebraska to the federal government in 1854. In 1872 he was deposed, then reinstated in 1873, though he was not an active chief from that time on.

In 1880, Arikíta insisted that his tribe wanted to move to the Indian Territory in Oklahoma. He said, "We have but one plan, . . . we want to move to Indian Territory. . . . It is hard to live here; whites are stealing our wood, you cannot find a good tree here; we want to go to Indian Territory to farm; we will live there together forever." In 1882 the Otoes moved to Indian Territory, where they shared reservations with the Ponca, the Pawnee, and the Missouri.

BIG BEAR, MISSOURIA CREE

ig Bear (Mistahimaskwa), born in 1825 near Fort Carleton in Saskatchewan, Canada, was a member of the Missouria Cree tribe. He became a chief of the Plains Cree in the 1870s, after he refused to sign a post-Confederation treaty with the Indians of Canada. When 2,000 members of the Cree tribe met at Chief Poundmaker's reserve, Big Bear stood before them and denounced the whites for dishonesty. He called on his people to stand united against their oppressors.

In 1885, Big Bear became one of the few chiefs of western Canada to lead his people in an uprising. He joined forces with the Metis, who were fighting to hold on to their land against white settlers. Warriors from Big Bear's band rode with the Metis, led by Chief Louis David Riel, and the Cree, led by Poundmaker, to raid a white settlement called Battleford. In the battle, nine settlers were killed.

The Canadian government sent Mounties and a special group of soldiers to put down the Crees and the Metis. Big Bear's band successfully resisted the soldiers' attacks several times, but finally on June 18, 1885, he released his white prisoners and sent a note with them asking for mercy. Once the government soldiers had all the Indians in captivity, they hanged eight rebel Indian leaders.

Big Bear and the Cree chief Poundmaker were sent to prison for three years. They were released early in 1887, but both died within six months of going free.

BIG ELK, OMAHA

ig Elk, or Ongpatonga, was born in 1765 into the Omaha tribe, who lived on the west banks of the Missouri River. He was probably born in a village that lay between what is today Omaha, Nebraska, and Sioux City, Iowa. He fought courageously as a young man in his tribe's war against the Pawnees. After the death of Black Bird in 1800, he became chief. He was his tribe's leader when the first sizable Euro-American migration—Mormons traveling to the shores of the Great Salt Lake—came through Omaha Territory. The Omaha never had any large-scale clashes with the whites; the tribe spent most of its time fighting the Dakotas.

A spellbinding speaker, Big Elk was also an outstanding diplomat. He signed two peace treaties in Washington, D.C., and while he was in the capital his portrait was painted twice, once by Charles Bird King, and later by George Catlin.

Big Elk was head chief of the Omahas for 43 years, until he was 78 years old. Out hunting alone, he killed a deer with a tomahawk, a rare event by that date, when most Native Americans hunted with guns. He died three days later, in 1843, from a fever. His burial place, in Bellevue, Nebraska, is called Elk Hill today.

Big Elk's son—Big Elk, Younger—succeeded him. In 1854, the Omaha sold their land to the U.S. government, except for one area that became their reservation.

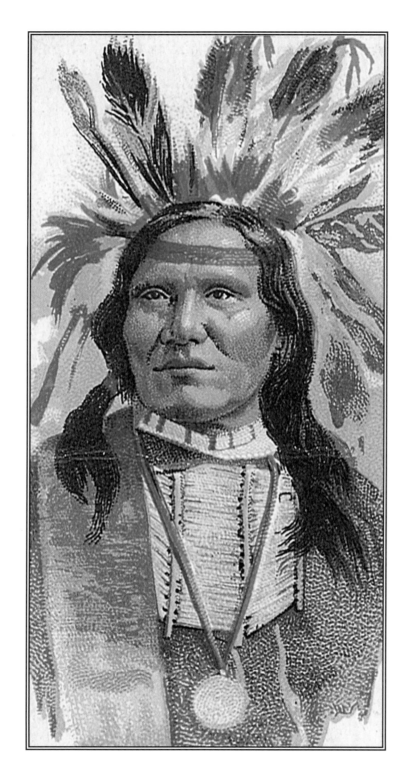

BIG SNAKE, PONCA

Big Snake of the Ponca tribe was murdered by American soldiers. The account of an eyewitness to the murder—Hairy Bear—appears in the book *Great Documents in American Indian History.*

Big Snake's tribe lived at the intersection of the Niobrara and Missouri Rivers in Nebraska. Between 1855 and 1868 the Poncas gave up enormous amounts of land to the federal government. Then in 1868 the government by mistake gave 96,000 acres of Ponca land to the Sioux, creating warfare between the two tribes. The U.S. Department of the Interior decided in 1876 to relocate the Ponca tribe to Indian Territory in Oklahoma.

Upon seeing the land in Oklahoma, Big Snake and his brother Standing Bear said no and walked the 500 miles back to Nebraska. But they were forced to return with their tribesmen to Oklahoma. Many Poncas died from disease and brutal conditions. By 1878, Standing Bear had lost both a daughter and his last living son.

In 1879 Standing Bear led a small band of Poncas back to Nebraska. There Big Snake decided to test the law that allowed the U.S. Army to forcibly move Native Americans onto reservations. He moved from his assigned Ponca Reservation to one occupied by the Cheyennes. When U.S. troops came to arrest him on October 31, 1879, he said he was innocent, for he hadn't understood the law. The agents saw that he carried no weapons. When they tried to forcibly move him from the sitting position he was in, he resisted. Six soldiers beat him with their rifle butts, then shot him to death. His brother Standing Bear remained in Nebraska, where he died in 1908.

BLACK HAWK, DAKOTA SIOUX

lack Hawk was a lesser known Dakota Sioux chief, outshone by his more famous fellow Dakota warrior chiefs Sitting Bull and Red Cloud. His tribe numbered around 25,000 in the late 17th century, when they lived in land that today is Minnesota and Wisconsin. During the 18th century, probably because of pressures from the Ojibwa tribe, one of the first tribes to obtain firearms, the Dakota Sioux moved onto the Great Plains and became nomadic buffalo hunters.

The name *Sioux* comes from an Ojibwa term meaning "adder" or "enemy." The Sioux called themselves Oceti Sakowin, which means "Seven Councils Fires," referring to their seven divisions.

Black Hawk was with Sitting Bull and Red Cloud at the signing of the Treaty of Laramie in 1868. Under its terms, the government would give the Sioux, along with members of the Cheyenne and Arapaho tribes, a large reservation that would include half of present-day South Dakota, and no white people would be allowed in the Powder River country.

Red Cloud and other chiefs accepted the agreement, but Sitting Bull refused to sign. He worried that it would diminish the ancestral range of the Sioux. It is believed that Black Hawk signed, though he wasn't pleased about it: "You have split my land and I don't like it. These lands once belonged to the Kiowas and the Crows, but we whipped these nations out of them, and in this we did what the white men do when they want the land of the Indians."

Although the government signed the treaty, the whites did not honor it.

Black Hawk, Sauk and Fox

lack Hawk, or Ma-ka-tai-me-she-kia-kiah, was a Sauk born in 1767 in what is now Rock Island, Illinois. His father, Pyesa, was keeper of the tribe's medicine bundle. After Pyesa died, Black Hawk became the keeper.

Black Hawk and his followers refused to accept the treaty of 1804, which allowed the Sauk to use all lands the Indians had turned over to the government, until the government sold them. But by 1828 the government demanded that all Indians leave Illinois.

In 1829, while Black Hawk and his people were out on their winter hunt, white settlers moved onto their land and even into their lodges. Still, Black Hawk refused to leave. In the meantime, White Cloud, a Winnebago, rallied many of his people to Black Hawk's cause. Black Hawk became more militant, counting on help from the British, with whom he had sided during the War of 1812. But his allies did not come to his aid.

He continued fighting on and off with the whites throughout the so-called Black Hawk War. On July 20, 1832, as he tried to surrender to the commander of the steamboat *Warrior,* many of Black Hawk's people were killed. The next day more were slaughtered by the army. The rest were charged with unprovoked aggression against the U.S. government and were forced to cede more land.

Black Hawk was imprisoned in Fort Monroe, Virginia. When he was allowed to return to his people, he was forbidden to act as their chief. He died at Iowaville in 1838.

CAYATANIA, NAVAJO

A member of the Navajo tribe, Cayatania, or Cayatanita, stayed in the shadow of his more famous brother, Manuelito, who was born in 1818.

Spanish explorers came upon the tribe in a part of Mexico that is now northern New Mexico during the 16th century and named them Navajo. Although there were many skirmishes with the Mexicans, and sometimes with other tribes, the Navajo mostly spent their time raising sheep, hunting wild game, and growing wheat, corn, and melons.

After the Spanish-American War in 1848, the U.S. govern-ment began making an effort to concentrate onto reservations all the Indian tribes in the territory it had won from Mexico.

The Navajo resisted, led by Cayatania and Manuelito, among others. Although the chiefs signed a treaty in 1858 agreeing to remain on the land the United States had designated for them, in 1860 they attacked Fort Defiance. Badly beaten, still they refused to surrender. To defeat them, Kit Carson started a scorched-earth campaign, destroying their livestock and burning their crops.

Finally, in March 1864 the 2,500 Navajo who surrendered were forced to trek to a new location, which turned out to be a wasteland near Fort Sumner. Many died en route. Not until 1866 did Manuelito and 23 of his surviving people surrender. He and Cayatania and others traveled to Washington, D.C., to plead with the government to let them return to their beloved land. In 1868 the Navaho were allowed to return home, but to a much smaller allotment of land than had been theirs for generations.

GALL, HUNKPAPA SIOUX

Gall was a Hunkpapa Sioux born in 1840 along the Moreau River in South Dakota. The story behind his name has been passed down: he tried to eat the gallbladder of an animal. He may have preferred a name he received as an adult, "The Fighting Cock of the Sioux."

Orphaned as a young child, Gall was adopted as a younger brother by Sitting Bull. He won a reputation as an outstanding warrior fighting Red Cloud's War for the Bozeman Trail between 1866 and 1868. Like Sitting Bull, he refused to give up his nomadic ways after the signing of the Fort Laramie Treaty.

Gall was Sitting Bull's primary strategist and field commander from 1876 to 1877 during the War for the Black Hills. He was partly responsible for the Indian victory over Col. George Armstrong Custer at the Battle of Little Bighorn; before that, Gen. George Crook had noticed his fighting skills at the Battle of Rosebud. These battles provoked massive retaliation by the U.S. government, which forced belligerent tribes onto reservations.

In the fall of 1880, Gall argued with Sitting Bull, and afterward took around 300 followers to Montana, where he decided to surrender to the government. By 1881, he was living on the Standing Rock Agency in North Dakota, where he supported agent James McLaughlin, whom he considered a friend. Sitting Bull was forced to live on the same reservation, but the two remained enemies.

Gall became an Episcopalian, appeared in Wild West shows, and later was an envoy to Washington, D.C. He became a judge of the Court of Indian Offenses, where he had a long-term impact on Native American standards.

GERONIMO, APACHE

Geronimo, or Gokhlayeh—"One Who Yawns" —was born in 1825 along the upper Gila River on what is today the Mexico-Arizona border. He belonged to the Chiricahua Apache tribe, whose name came from the Zuni word *apachu,* meaning "enemy."

In a fight against the Mexicans who had killed his mother, wife, and three children in 1858, Geronimo established his reputation as a fierce and powerful warrior. He enlisted the help of fellow Apache Cochise and Chief Juh of the Nednis to get his revenge. During their attack on the Mexican stronghold of Arizpe, a Mexican soldier shouted, "Geronimo!"—Spanish for Jerome—after watching him in battle, and the name stuck. (Why the man shouted that name, or whom he was shouting at, remains a mystery.)

Geronimo then placed himself under the leadership of Cochise, who was also warring against whites. The two spent a decade in revengeful warfare until Cochise died in 1872.

The U.S. government continued forcing the Chiricahua to join other Apaches in the Southwest Indian territories, and Geronimo continued to refuse to go. Famous as the ultimate Native American holdout, he and his followers became renegades for the next ten years, returning to the reservation, then escaping again and terrorizing the whites. One white officer was so furious that he exiled all the Apaches on the reservations to Florida. Finally, 5,000 soldiers were ordered to subdue Geronimo and the 39 Apaches with him.

Geronimo surrendered when he learned his people had been sent to Florida. He was imprisoned for two years, then sent out as a human exhibit to events such as the St. Louis World's Fair in 1904. He died in 1909, a broken old man.

HENRY BULL HEAD, SIOUX

hen 43 policemen were ordered to arrest the great Sioux chief Sitting Bull just before daybreak on December 15, 1890, they were led by Lt. Henry Bull Head, a Sioux policeman.

Although Sitting Bull then lived in a small cabin on the Standing Rock Reservation, he continued to wield great influence over his tribesmen. He frustrated the agents who were in charge of the reservation—he resisted their attempts to convert the Sioux to Christianity, he refused to take only one wife, and he insisted that the medicine men be allowed to practice.

In 1889, a young Paiute mystic named Wovoka had claimed that he saw visions of change that offered hope to the trapped Native Americans. In one vision, he saw that the Native Americans would be restored to their natural heritage. Wovoka encouraged all Indians to dance regularly so they might "die" and gain a glimpse of the paradise to come. Many dancers said they went into trances and saw old ancestors. Whites called the practice the "ghost dance religion." Its focus on resurrection and reunion with the dead made them nervous.

The federal agent James McLaughlin, who had never liked Sitting Bull, reported that he was the "high priest" of the ghost dance movement. McLaughlin sent Lieutenant Henry Bull Head to arrest the chief. When the 44 police approached Sitting Bull, one of his followers shot Bull Head, badly wounding him. Bull Head shot Sitting Bull as he fell, and another policeman finished the old chief off. When the shooting was over, six policemen and eight of Sitting Bull's followers were dead.

IRON BULL, CROW

Iron Bull was a member of the Crow tribe, originally called *Absaroke,* or "The Bird People." The French called them "Crow People," and the name stuck. These were a proud people who at one time were recorded as having more than 10,000 horses. They felt a strong contempt for the whites who kept encroaching on their territory, and the tribe was constantly at war with the Dakotas.

In a book published in 1877, *Cheyenne Memories,* Iron Bull's people and encampment were described by an enthusiastic young army lieutenant as carefree and joyous. Lieutenant Scott remembered well the chief's dark, great lodge, whose coolness offered such a contrast to the heat of the army tents.

In the 1870s, with his career as a warrior behind him, Iron Bull followed tribe member Wolf Bow, the first Crow to settle permanently on a reservation, to learn how to farm. Chiefs Plenty Coups and Pretty Eagle were soon farming nearby. In 1884 the U.S. government forced all the Crow natives to move onto the floor of the Little Bighorn Valley, where they established the town of Crow Agency. They were going home, but to a way of life entirely different from the hunting life they had lived for so long.

The St. Xavier mission, established by Father Prando, was built close to Iron Bull's home. Shortly before he died, Iron Bull was urging his Crow neighbors to take up farming and convert to Christianity.

JOHN GRASS, TEON SIOUX

ohn Grass was born about 1837. His original name was Mato Watakpe, which means "Charging Bear." His father was Grass, or Old Grass, leader of the Sihasapa Sioux during the Sioux Wars of the 1860s and 1870s. John Grass was a Teon Sioux chief whose name is associated not with war but with diplomacy.

During the later struggles between the whites and Native Americans, John Grass was a diplomat under federal agent James McLaughlin. McLaughlin tried to use Grass and Chief Gall to tarnish the prestige and weaken the power of Sitting Bull, when he was brought to the Standing Rock Agency. McLaughlin failed.

From Sioux warrior and hunter, Grass became a hard-working Christian farmer. Whites pointed to him as a shining example of an Indian who had adapted to their way of life. What had replaced the once-mighty warrior societies of the Plains Indians was an Indian police force, tribe members loyal to white authorities who were expected to keep order on the government's behalf. Grass was instrumental in 1889 in getting other chiefs to sign the agreement that led to the division of the Great Sioux Reservation into four smaller tracts, which earned him the enmity of Sitting Bull forever.

After Chief Gall died, John Grass became the most commanding figure in the Sioux nation. He was one of the chiefs who negotiated a settlement after the tragic massacre of Native Americans at Wounded Knee. For years chief justice at the Standing Rock Indian Agency, he was admired for his eloquence and diplomacy. He died in 1918.

JOSEPH, NEZ PERCE

The Nez Perce chief Joseph spoke to his son, Joseph the Younger, from his deathbed in 1871. "My son, never forget my dying words. This country holds your father's body. Never sell the bones of your father or mother."

The old chief was baptized in 1836 by a Presbyterian minister and named Joseph after he showed interest in the teachings of the missionaries. His son, Chief Joseph, also called Hin-mah-too-Yah-lat-kekt—"Thunder Rolling in the Mountain"—was born in Wallowa Valley, Oregon, around 1840.

Chief Joseph the Younger was six feet tall and powerfully built. His life was quite peaceful until the 1870s, when a gold rush in Idaho led the whites to reduce Indian holdings. Chief Joseph refused to sign a treaty giving away seven million acres to the whites, which caused a split in the tribe between the Christian Nez Perce and the non-Christian. From then on, Chief Joseph and his followers were known as the nontreaty Nez Perce.

In 1877 several Nez Perce warriors went on a raid, killing 21 whites. In a fierce battle that followed, Chief Joseph and his bands defeated the soldiers who had come after them. In what would be called the Nez Perce Indian War, the Nez Perces covered over 1,000 miles, outfighting and outmaneuvering the soldiers who pursued them across Montana, only to suffer defeat a few miles from refuge in Canada. The 414 who were left surrendered.

Chief Joseph finished out his life on the Colville Reservation in Washington, where he died on September 21, 1904.

KEOKUK, SAUK AND FOX

eokuk, or "One Who Moves About Alert," never killed an enemy but became a chief of the Fox tribe because of his way with words.

The Fox and Sauk at first fought together against the whites. (They are often thought of as one tribe, but they had a close alliance rather than a confederacy.) When the Treaty of St. Louis was signed, however, giving away 50 million acres of Indian land to the U.S. government, the tribes split. Two chiefs became associated with this rift: Keokuk, a Fox, and Black Hawk, a Sauk.

When new conflicts arose with the Americans after the War of 1812, Keokuk began to pull away from Black Hawk and argue for friendship with the Americans. Black Hawk, forced by the Americans to move across the Mississippi, continued fighting. Now Keokuk openly supported the Americans, and he and Black Hawk remained rivals. In 1816, after the peace treaty between the United States and Great Britain, they agreed never to reunite their bands.

The government appointed Keokuk chief of the Sauk in 1843. Along with two other Sauk and Fox chiefs, Keokuk ceded the Rock River land area to the United States. Eventually, they ceded six million acres of some of the richest soil in the world on the Iowa side of the Mississippi.

Keokuk was an eloquent speaker, and in his later years, he became famous for his splendid dress. When he and his followers went to Washington, D.C., they marched down the streets wearing buckskins and buffalo robes. Keokuk rode to visit neighboring tribes dressed in beautiful skins, surrounded by 50 bodyguards, as though he were royalty. Chief Keokuk died in 1848 in Kansas.

LEAN WOLF, GROS VENTRE

At the Library of Congress in Washington, D.C., you can see a map that Lean Wolf drew, tracing a route he took in a successful raid for Sioux horses.

Lean Wolf was a member of one of the twelve bands that made up the Gros Ventre ("Big Belly"), or Algonquian tribe. The groups separated in the winter to follow the buffalo, and in summer, they came back together to perform the celebration of the Sun Dance and to hunt buffalo, which they surrounded on horseback. The women made buffalo-skin tipis and cut up the buffalo meat and dried it on racks. They filled out the tribe's diet with berries, birds' eggs, rhubarb, and other foods found in the wild, and they made clothing from deer or elk skin.

The bands camped in a large circle with an opening facing east, with each band assigned to a certain area. The Gros Ventre would sometimes move camp six or eight times in a summer. They pulled tipis and other belongings behind dog or horse travois, and when they came to a river, they built a raft. Girls of this tribe married at age 11 or 12, usually to an older man. It wasn't unusual for men to have more than one wife, and divorce was common.

The Gros Ventre fought the Crow alongside the Blackfoot during the mid-19th century, but in 1867 their loyalties reversed and they joined the Crow to fight the Blackfoot. They remained friendly with the Arapaho, Cheyenne, and Cree and fought the Shoshoni and Flathead.

They were moved to the Fort Belknap Reservation in Montana in the 1880s.

MAD BEAR, LOWER YANKTONA SIOUX

ad Bear probably fought alongside Sitting Bull in the Battle of Little Bighorn, defeating Col. George Armstrong Custer. We do not know whether Mad Bear then joined Sitting Bull in exile in Canada in 1876, but he probably did participate in the ghost dance that brought together the Sioux tribes in one last rebellion against the white man.

Most of the tribes of the Sioux nation became known as the Dakota Sioux. Dakota became "Nakota" for the Yanktons and "Lakota" for the Teton Sioux. The most famous and powerful of the Teton Sioux chiefs was Sitting Bull. Mad Bear was a Lower Yanktona Sioux.

The Sioux ghost dancers believed in a new messiah, a Sioux Indian who would come soon and chase the white invaders away. They also believed that the more participants in the ghost dance, the faster the messiah would come. The frenzy of the dancing turned into outright insurrection and ended with the massacre of the Sioux at Wounded Knee and the death of Sitting Bull in 1890.

But Mad Bear, who once had hoped for deliverance by the Sioux messiah, had sold out long before. When the time came to accept the price the government wanted to pay for the lands, he signed any documents the agency told him to. He and Chiefs Gall, Charging Bear, and others had accepted the white culture foisted upon them by the Bureau of Indian Affairs. The Sioux's social and religious rites were forbidden and their dances closely supervised. Children came home from school with their hair cut short. There was no more hunting and gathering of food. Parents had to collect food rations from the agency.

Man Chief, Pawnee

The most heroic act of Man Chief's life may have occurred when he was only 20 years old and took a stand against his own Pawnee customs to save the life of an enemy Sioux maiden.

Pawnee myth and folklore were highly symbolic. Their religion was full of rituals and visions. Each year the tribe sacrificed a young woman to the morning-star deity, in a ritual called the Morning Star Ceremony. But in 1817, Man Chief's father, Knife Chief, one of the leaders of the Pawnee tribe, got to know William Clark, superintendent of Indian Affairs in St. Louis. Clark told him about the white man's religion, and Knife Chief began to question his tribe's rites of human sacrifice. His son did more than question.

When Man Chief (or Petalesharro) went against tribal custom by preventing the sacrifice of a Sioux girl, he risked his life because the Pawnee believed that interfering with the sacred Morning Star Ceremony would bring certain death. Stories of Man Chief's bravery spread, and in the fall of 1821 he went to Washington, D.C., to receive a reward.

Even then, the sacrifices did not end completely. Despite opposition from government agents and chiefs, a woman was sacrificed in 1833. The last recorded Pawnee sacrifice was that of a Lakota girl in 1838.

Ancient enemies of the Sioux, the Pawnee lived in the area that is now Nebraska, in four distinct bands, each with its own chief. They lived in earth lodges in villages and were farmers as well as warriors. In the late 19th century, some half century after the sacrifices ended, the tribe exchanged all the land they had left for a reservation in Oklahoma. Fewer than 100 Pawnees then remained alive.

MOSES, FOX

oses was the favorite son of the Fox chief Keokuk. He spoke Algonquian and ate his berries laced with maple syrup, which was a staple in his tribe's diet. Moses and Keokuk were Fox Indians and they belonged to the Bear Clan. The Fox lived in the woodlands of the Northeast and the Great Lakes. They moved with the seasons around the fertile area between Lake Michigan, Rock River, and the Mississippi River.

Among the Fox, each clan had a spiritual ancestor, an animal or mythical being, and the clan members considered themselves its relatives. Like their neighboring tribes and relatives, the Fox always chose their peacetime leader from one particular clan. For the Fox, that was the Bear Clan. So when the Fox chose Moses as their chief, he, like his father, drew his power from his spiritual ancestor, the Great Ancestral Bear.

As splendid in his dress as his father, Moses Keokuk, accompanied by other tribe leaders, wore bear-claw necklaces when he visited Washington, D.C., on a peace mission in 1867. Moses carried a tomahawk and an arrow in his hand and wore his hair combed straight back and up with a large eagle feather stuck in it. Instead of his standard animal-skin vest symbolizing the Bear clan, he wore a mid-thigh striped tunic with puffed sleeves.

RED BIRD, WINNEBAGO

Dressed in white fringed buckskin, with half his face painted red, the other half green and white, Chief Red Bird of the Winnebago tribe bravely entered the tent where the white men were gathered singing his death song. He sat down and quietly lit his pipe. To save his people and end the Winnebago War of 1827, he was turning himself in. Two years later he died in prison.

The Winnebagos lived in present-day Wisconsin. The tribe, like many of its neighbors, resisted the intrusion of white settlers onto their land. They had an added burden— miners came for the rich lead deposits on Winnebago land, the upper Mississippi country of northwest Illinois and southwest Wisconsin.

In 1826 some Winnebagos killed a white family near Prairie du Chien. The next year, after suffering a number of assaults by whites on their tribe, leaders in the western Winnebago villages chose Red Bird to take revenge. He was reluctant, but finally he and a couple of companions attacked a French household, killing and wounding several people.

The incident that triggered the Winnebago Uprising also happened near Prairie du Chien. Some white men, after drinking rum with some Winnebago tribesmen, kidnapped several Winnebago women. The Indians followed them and attacked a few days later. The Americans descended with a huge show of force, ready to retaliate. Red Bird's dramatic surrender impressed the whites, who did not kill him but sent him and other Winnebagos to prison. There in 1829 they signed a document that allowed white miners to continue working their land and ceded the tribe's territory south of the Wisconsin River to the government.

RED CLOUD, OGLALA SIOUX

ed Cloud's name comes from the crimson clouds that drifted over the western horizon on the day he was born in 1820. By the time this Oglala Sioux chief died 89 years later, in 1909, his name was synonymous with the Bozeman Trail War, often referred to as "Red Cloud's War."

The Powder River country, a hunter's paradise, was guaranteed to the Sioux by treaty in 1851. But in 1862 the federal government tried to force the Sioux to allow John M. Bozeman to carve out a route through their hunting grounds to connect the gold fields in Montana to the east. To help Bozeman push through the Sioux lands, Gen. Patrick E. Connor stormed into Red Cloud's territory in 1865, but the Sioux and their allies overwhelmed his troops.

Next, the government tried the peace process. A commission arrived with a peace treaty, but none of the Powder River chiefs would sign, because Colonel Carrington with 700 troops had just arrived on Sioux land to build forts. Red Cloud recruited 3,000 warriors, who began a relentless attack on Colonel Carrington's people. John Bozeman was killed in 1867 on his own road by Blackfoot warriors.

When the government approached Red Cloud again with a treaty, he refused to sign anything until all forts were gone. Finally, Congress decided to give up. The Bozeman Trail was closed, and on November 6, 1868, Red Cloud signed the Sioux Treaty of 1868 at Fort Laramie.

He went to Washington, D.C., in 1870, where he managed to get future concessions for his people. But articles in the treaty that had not been explained to him caused his people to eventually become "reservation Indians."

RED THUNDER, YANKTONA SIOUX

 **C**hief of a band of the Yanktona Sioux in the early 1800s, Red Thunder was also known as Shappa ("The Beaver"). Lt. Zebulon M. Pike thought him the most beautifully dressed chief to appear at the council at Prairie du Chien, Wisconsin, in 1808. The Yanktona were one of the seven main divisions of the Dakota. They had come to the Plains of the Iowas and the Dakotas in the early 1700s.

The United States declared war on Britain on June 18, 1812. Many Native Americans sided with the British in this war, the War of 1812, because of an American insult. In the 1809 Treaty of Fort Wayne, the Americans offered the Fox, Sauk, and Winnebago tribes $7,000 for their land, plus a certain amount every year. This puny offer enraged the Native Americans.

Red Thunder and his son Waneta fought with the British, earning recognition for their valor at the battles of Fort Meig and Sandusky, Ohio. Waneta went on to earn a U.S. captain's commission and to visit England.

British general Henry Proctor, who viewed Native Americans as untutored savages, eventually betrayed them. He abandoned them and Fort Malden, a British stronghold, to American forces. This left the Native Americans with no chance of driving the Americans off their land, or in fact reclaiming what was theirs.

Red Thunder's son Waneta switched to the U.S. side sometime after 1820 and was one of the signers of the treaty of Prairie du Chien, which established the boundaries of Sioux territory. Red Thunder was killed by the Chippewa in 1823 on the Red River.

SITTING BULL, DAKOTA SIOUX

 itting Bull was more than just a great warrior. He was also a singer and songwriter and a mystic who was said to be able to communicate with animals. By 1867, he was chief of several Sioux bands.

After Gen. George Crook attacked a Cheyenne village in 1876, Sitting Bull and Cheyenne chief Crazy Horse combined forces to fight the whites. More than 10,000 Indians headed toward the Rosebud and Little Bighorn Rivers. A vision had shown Sitting Bull that the Indians would be victorious. The Battle of Little Bighorn, often called "Custer's Last Stand," took place on June 25, 1876. Col. George Armstrong Custer and his men were killed.

It was Sitting Bull's final victory. Many tribal chiefs began surrendering to the whites, but Sitting Bull said that before he would consider peace the whites must agree that he would not sell any part of his country and they must quit cutting timber on his land and abandon their forts.

After Chief Crazy Horse was stabbed to death, some Cheyenne followed Sitting Bull to Canada. Because food was scarce and he had no support from Canadian officials, he returned to the United States in May 1881, where he eventually ended up on the Standing Rock Reservation. There he was made to participate in Buffalo Bill's Wild West Show.

The government took away more of Sitting Bull's land in the Sioux Act of 1889. Sitting Bull went to Washington but he failed to negotiate better terms. When Sitting Bull took up a new religion and began dancing the ghost dance army agents grew nervous. One agent, James McLaughlin, sent in Sioux police to arrest Sitting Bull. A fight followed, and Sitting Bull and his son were killed.

SPOTTED TAIL, BRULE SIOUX

potted Tail, or Sinte Gleska, acquired his name from a fur trader's gift to him—a raccoon tail. He was a Brule Sioux warrior who fought many battles with the Pawnee and later became a skilled negotiator.

He was born around 1823 near Fort Laramie, Wyoming. In 1854, he and his warriors attacked a group of soldiers who had entered their camp to investigate a settler's complaint that a Brule had stolen his cow. Spotted Tail and his warriors killed all the soldiers. Gen. William S. Harney retaliated in 1855, killing 86 Brules and taking 70 prisoners, including Spotted Tail's wife and infant daughter. Spotted Tail later surrendered but, to his shock, was released.

Spotted Tail became the chief spokesman for the Brule bands. Realizing that military victory for the Indians was unlikely, he urged his people to accommodate the whites.

President Ulysses S. Grant had ordered that all Indians be placed on reservations run by Indian agencies by January 1, 1876. After Sitting Bull's victory at Little Bighorn in 1876, Spotted Tail was appointed chief of the Sioux. In 1877, he was one of the negotiators of the Sioux surrender, for which many Sioux resented him.

Spotted Tail learned to speak English. He wanted to preserve Sioux culture, but he also understood that his children would need to learn English in order to help their people. He sent four sons and two grandchildren to the Carlisle Indian School in Pennsylvania, then removed them when he learned the school had baptized them into the Christian faith and given them English names.

Spotted Tail was killed on August 5, 1881, by a Sioux subchief.

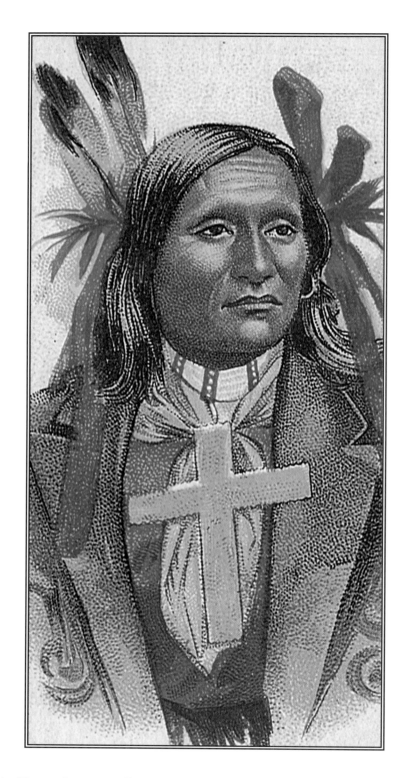

White Shield, Southern Cheyenne

hite Shield, or Wopohwats, was born into the Southern Cheyenne tribe in 1833 in what is now Wyoming. The Cheyenne were warriors known for their great height and their courage and intelligence, who fought the whites from 1860 to 1878. After they were defeated by Col. George Armstrong Custer in 1868, they joined with several Sioux bands and took revenge on the whites during the battle at Little Bighorn, when Custer and all his men were killed.

White Shield grew up fighting the Pawnees but became a pacifist during the 1860s, declaring that he wanted peace with the whites. He was elected to the Cheyenne council of chiefs in 1870 and the following year was sent to Washington, D.C., as a tribal delegate. While there, he met Ulysses S. Grant.

He settled his band on the North Canadian River in the Indian Territory and managed to keep his band at peace when some Cheyennes, along with the Comanches and Kiowas, were part of the Red River Wars of 1874–1875.

In the 1890s the government organized Native American police forces as a means of breaking down tribal authority. They were usually men who knew the language and the country. It was a difficult job, for they were often not respected by their own people. White Shield became a police captain. Little has been discovered about his politics, except that he openly oppposed leasing Indian grasslands to white cattlemen.

White Shield had a son, Harvey White Shield, who became a mission teacher and interpreter after attending the Carlisle School in Pennsylvania.

WHITE SWAN, CROW

embers of the Crow tribe provided the U.S. Army with outstanding trackers, whom they called scouts, between 1850 and 1880. White Swan was a scout who served under Col. George Armstrong Custer at the Battle of Little Bighorn in 1876.

In 1874 Custer was ordered by Gen. William T. Sherman to lead an expedition into the Black Hills to report on the status of the Indians there. Many gold prospectors went with him, and they received permission to stay in South Dakota at their own risk.

By 1875, the Sioux—a confederation of seven Native American tribes—were finding conditions on their reservation so bad that many of their people were leaving. The Department of the Interior ordered them to return to their reservations by January 31, 1876. The Sioux, under leaders Sitting Bull, Gall, and Crazy Horse, ignored the order and set up a camp on the Little Bighorn River. The U.S. Army took over and sent in troops from three directions.

The Indians attacked Gen. George Crook's men first, delaying his meeting with the other army leaders. Gen. Alfred H. Terry ordered Custer to go up the Rosebud River to fight the Sioux there. Custer came upon approximately 2,000 warriors on June 25, 1876, and ordered an attack. He was so outnumbered, he soon moved to higher ground. But he had underestimated both the Native Americans' numbers and their ability to fight—he and his 225 men were killed by the Sioux.

White Swan was badly crippled during the battle but he did not die until 1905. He is buried in the national cemetery at the Custer battlefield in Montana.

CHRONOLOGY

1763   Royal Proclamation of 1763 issued by British king George III establishes boundary lines: Native Americans have the right to use all land outside established colonies until land-cession treaties are negotiated.

1778   First U.S.-Indian Treaty, between the United States and the Delaware tribe.

1786   First federal Indian reservation established.

1789   Bureau of Indian Affairs moved to War Department.

1803   Louisiana Purchase adds a large Indian population to the United States.

1806–1809   To halt westward expansion of U.S. settlers, Tecumseh and Tenskwatawa try to unite Native American peoples.

1809   Treaty of Fort Wayne: the Delaware, Potawatomi, Miami, Kickapoo, and Eel River tribes give up around 3 million acres of land for $8,200.

1823   U.S. Supreme Court rules that Indians can grant land only to the federal government, but they have the right to land by prior use.

1830   Congress passes Indian Removal Act.

1835–1841   Second Seminole War.

1846–1848   Mexican-American War.

1850–1880   Genocide of California Indians.

1853–1856   U.S. acquires 174 million acres of Indian lands through 52 treaties.

1861–1863	Apache uprisings under Cochise and Mangas Colorado.
1861–1865	U.S. Civil War
1866–1868	War for the Bozeman Trail in Wyoming and Montana under Chief Red Cloud.
1868	Treaty of Fort Laramie resolves the Bozeman Trail conflict. Creation of Navajo Indian Reservation. Sioux Treaty of 1868.
1870	U.S. Supreme Court rules that Indians are not citizens of the United States.
1871	U.S. formally ends treaty-making with Native American tribes.
1874–1875	The Red River (Buffalo) Wars.
1874–1881	Warfare on the northern Plains.
1876	Battle of Little Bighorn.
1879	Carlisle Indian School founded in Pennsylvania to assimilate Indians into white culture.
1881–1885	President Chester A. Arthur approves rules forbidding Indian "rites, customs . . . contrary to civilization."
1882	U.S. Congress creates "Indian Territory."
1886	Apache resistance under Geronimo.
1890	Wounded Knee massacre.
1924	Indians become U.S. citizens.

INDEX ᴥ

FURTHER READING

Capps, Benjamin. *The Great Chiefs.* New York: Time-Life Books, 1975.

Dockstader, Frederick J. *Great North American Indians.* Boston: Houghton Mifflin, 1996.

Dunn, John M. *The Relocation of the North American Indian.* Lucent, 1995.

Edmunds, R. David, ed. *American Indian Leaders: Studies in Diversity.* Lincoln: University of Nebraska Press, 1980.

Fleming, Paula Richardson, and Judith Luskey. *The North American Indians in Early Photographs.* New York: Barnes & Noble, 1986.

Hoxie, Frederick E., ed. *Encyclopedia of North American Indians.* Boston: Houghton-Mifflin, 1996.

Johansen, Bruce E., and Donald A. Grinde, Jr. *The Encyclopedia of Native American Biography.* New York: Holt, 1997.

Time-Life Books. *The Reservations.* New York: Time-Life Books, 1995.

Time-Life Books. *The Mighty Chieftains.* New York: Time-Life Books, 1993.

Trigger, Bruce G. *Handbook of North American Indians: Northeast.* Washington, D.C.: Smithsonian Institution Press, 1978.

Utley, Robert M., and Wilcomb E. Washburn. *The American Heritage History of the Indian Wars.* New York: American Heritage, 1977.

Waldman, Carl. *Atlas of the North American Indian.* New York: Facts on File, 1985.